The Circle for Tallulah Falls School Presents

Southern Occasions

AN INSIDER'S LOOK AT SOUTHERN HOSPITALITY

COMMUNICATION CHANNELS/BUSINESS ATLANTA

FIRST ATLANTA

WESTIN PEACHTREE PLAZA

Produced By:
MARILYN M. LONG, MARIANNE BROADBEAR, AND CAROLYN LEE WILLS

Photographed By:
DWIGHT HOWARD PHOTOGRAPHER

Published By:
PERRY COMMUNICATIONS, INC.

Designer:
MARK ROKFALUSI

Editorial Assistance:
SUSAN HUNTER PUBLISHING

BENEFITTING TALLULAH FALLS SCHOOL

INTRODUCTION

Company in our homes is a natural way of life to Southerners. This book welcomes you to the gracious homes of twenty Atlanta families to share a year of their Southern Occasions. You'll read about their homes and feast your eyes on the exciting decor and fabulous food they served their guests.

You'll get recipes and tips from the hostesses on creating memorable occasions, from intimate dinner parties to cocktail buffets, to backyard barbecues and grand formal receptions.

So visit these homes to enjoy the abundant spirit of Southern entertaining at its festive, most creative best. Sample home-cooked specialties and warm hospitality. See the artistry of hostesses, caterers, florists, architects, and decorators whose work has been so beautifully photographed and presented on these pages. Learn why Southern hospitality is famous the world over.

Welcome!

Nathalie Dupree

Nathalie Dupree

ACKNOWLEDGEMENTS

This book was conceived and written by members of the Circle for Tallulah Falls School. The purpose of the Circle is the support of Tallulah Falls Schools. The proceeds from the sale of this book will go toward scholarships and school improvements.

Previously the Circle had published a successful cookbook, *Culinary Classics,* which sold out at over 16,000 copies. When the fund raising committee sought a new project, committee members Marilyn Long, Carolyn Lee Wills, and Marianne Broadbear looked to the particular talents of Circle members for inspiration. One apparent talent was entertaining, and so the committee suggested publishing a beautiful book to showcase and share the party-giving talents of the members.

The idea for the book was begun during the presidency of Carolyn Lee Wills. Nathalie Dupree, Southern food authority, cookbook author, and host of PBS's *New Southern Cooking,* helped crystalize the idea. We received sage publishing advice from Marge McDonald of Marmac Publishing. The idea was approved and photography began under the presidency of Liz Sudderth.

Perry Communications, Inc. agreed to publish the book and provide financial backing. We are especially grateful for the faith Tommy Walker of Perry Communications has shown in our project, and for the guidance of Perry's Fred Brown, the former publisher of *Brown's Guide to Georgia,* who kept us on track.

This book was photographed by Dwight Howard assisted by his sons Dwight, Jr. and Cliff. Twenty Circle members hosted wonderful parties—real parties, not staged events—and shared their skills and time. We appreciate the photographers, the book committee members, and Fred Brown for giving up their holidays all year to attend the parties and capture their hospitable spirit for this book. Harry Burke embossed the cover and deserves a special thanks for all the help he has given the Circle over the years.

The final photography, production, and prepublication work were completed during the presidency of Lynn Wright, with additional sales done under the presidency of Peggy Fulghum.

We are grateful to our sponsors: First Atlanta, The Westin Peachtree Plaza, and Communication Channels/Business Atlanta, for their confidence in our idea and our abilities. We say thank you to them, the gracious hosts and guests of all the parties, and all the wonderful, supportive people involved.

We hope you enjoy the beautiful interiors and delicious recipes of our Southern Occasions. We are pleased to share our hospitality and our ideas for elegant entertaining for the benefit of a worthy cause.

Marilyn M. Long

Carolyn Lee Wills

Marianne Broadbear

CONTENTS

CHRISTMAS COCKTAIL BUFFET
2

NEW YEAR'S DAY BRUNCH
7

WILD GAME SUPER BOWL PARTY
14

LUNCH FOR THE LADIES
19

BABY SHOWER LUNCHEON
25

EASTER EGG HUNT
31

BAR MITZVAH
38

THANK YOU PARTY
43

RETIREMENT SALUTE
50

VICTORIAN HOUSE BLESSING
55

FRENCH MUSICAL TRIBUTE
61

A MIDSUMMER'S EVENING
68

WEDDING RECEPTION
73

FOURTH OF JULY JUBILEE
80

SOUTHERN BIRTHDAY BARBECUE
85

GOLDEN WEDDING ANNIVERSARY
91

ELECTION CELEBRATION DINNER
98

THANKSGIVING FAMILY FEAST
103

THE NIGHT BEFORE CHRISTMAS
110

IDEAS: WHAT HELPS AND
WHAT MAKES A PARTY SPECIAL
116

EPILOGUE: LOOKING BACK AT
TALLULAH FALLS SCHOOL AND THE CIRCLE
119

Published by the Circle For Tallulah Falls School. Printed in the United States by Perry Communications, 2181 Sylvan Road SW, Atlanta, Georgia 30344.

ISBN 0-9624452-0-7

*A tree this beautiful takes time and planning.
The over 2000 lights take 16 hours to apply before
other decorating even begins.*

Jann and Bob Kern's home is always special at Christmas. For over a decade, they have chosen the Christmas season to share their warmth and hospitality with friends and business associates.

The Kerns' traditional Christmas party started with a small group of friends but has enlarged each year until there are nearly 150 names on the guest list. To help her

The Kern's Italian Renaissance style home is next door to the Georgia Governor's Mansion in Buckhead.

make Christmas decorating easier as well as more spectacular (it takes sixteen hours to put the 2,000 lights on the tree), Jann retains the services of Yevette Callahan of Festive Holiday Decor. To make the party particularly memorable, the Kerns plan the menu carefully with Rowland's Catering so they have a feast of a meal and excellent service.

The evening includes cocktails, piano music, a tempting buffet, and the warm hospitality that is a trademark of the Kerns' entertaining. The dessert table is sumptuous, causing guests to put aside thoughts of dieting and calorie counting for the night. The evening puts the twinkle in Christmas and lets every guest share the Christmas spirit.

Villa Juanita was built between 1922 and 1924 for newlyweds Julia Gatins Murphy and Conkey Pate Whitehead. Conkey was the son of J.B. Whitehead, Sr., a principal founder of the Coca-Cola bottling industry and president of the Atlanta Coca-Cola Bottling Company at the time of his death in 1906. Julia's father, John E. Murphy, was president of the Lowery National Bank, which later became Atlanta's Trust Company Bank.

Mrs. Whitehead lived at Villa Juanita until her death in the 1930s. She left the property to her sister, Katherine Riley, who lived there fifty years. After Ms. Riley's death in 1985, Jann and Bob Kern bought the house. Located next door to Georgia's Governor's Mansion, the Kerns were determined not only to restore it, but to give it a new feeling of light and space. The Kerns removed walls, opened up the back of the house, landscaped, and added a pool in the same shape as the fish pond it replaced.

Special furnishings include a 1725 French chest in the master bedroom and a Baccarat crystal inkwell, a Christmas present to Jann from Bob. The living room fireplace looks like chunks of firelight captured in marble. Beneath the mantel is a classical bas-relief of young boys carrying a boar's head.

Chairs and sofas throughout the house are peppered with needlepoint and petit-point pillows. Erte sculptures and contemporary art punctuate the decor. To allow more light, knotted draperies are used as borders for the arched windows. Warm woods and bright colors were used to create a house that is comfortable and functional for the Kerns and their guests.

The dramatic two story entrance hall (above) sets the style for the rest of the home. Real foliage has been mixed with artificial garland and decorations to eliminate the problem of shedding while maintaining the authentic feel of decorations from Christmas past.

2

The merriment of Christmas is captured and spread with the singing of Christmas Carols.

Kristmas at the Kern's
Cocktails and Dinner
Date   Time
Villa Juanita
RSVP

*The spectacular Christmas decorations were done by
Yvette Callahan. Each one shows a special touch making
the whole house alive with the spirit of Christmas.*

The dramatic presentation of food and flowers adds to the splendor and beauty of the Christmas decor.

No guest could possibly resist this sinful dessert buffet.

M • E • N • U
SEAFOOD MORNAY
MINIATURE QUICHE
APRICOT STUFFED BAKED BRIE
CRUDITES WITH HOT BACON DIP
PORK TENDERLOIN WITH APRICOT OR JEZEBEL SAUCE
GRILLED ORIENTAL CHICKEN
SCALLOPS WRAPPED IN BACON
CRAB "ROWLAND" ON TOASTED BAGUETTE ROLLS
DECAF. CHOCOLATE ALMOND COFFEE w/WHIPPED CREAM & CHOCOLATE SHAVINGS
APPLE STRUDEL PIE
CHOCOLATE SUICIDE CAKE
CHOCOLATE MOUSSE CAKE   COOKIES

Among the many treats produced by Rowland's catering was this decadent Chocolate Mousse Cake.

Left to right, Stephen Baker, Kathy Baker, Bob Kern, and Jann Kern are having a hard time making choices from this lavish buffet (right).

The symmetry of the Long's traditional French style home disguises the nontraditional interior. Architect, Bob Whitfield, was instrumental in making it all work.

The New Year's Day Brunch tradition at the home of Marilyn and Noah Long began when 40 friends and neighbors gathered in 1974. Now 75 to 100 guests anticipate the annual event where they enjoy the traditional New Year's Day menu of blackeyed peas and ham, plus brunch fare that includes jambalaya, eggs, bacon, and cheese grits.

Marilyn and Noah Long, along with their sons Gregg and Cary, do all of the preparation, spending most of New Year's Eve in the kitchen cooking, setting up, and watching football games. This tradition has made the New Year's holiday a family time for the Longs. It's a personal celebration they enjoy more each year.

The reindeer theme for the holiday decorations is inspired by a book. A first edition of *Rudolph The Rednosed Reindeer* was given to Marilyn when she was four years old. It is signed by the author, Robert L. May, who wrote the book as a promotion for Montgomery Ward department stores.

Guests bring their dreams for the New Year: feelings of renewal, hope and optimism; no one comes without a smile. Anyone who overindulges on New Year's Eve finds this brunch is the cure.

Because Marilyn collects lions and Noah collects eagles, they named their house "Griffin Court" as a combination of the two. Designed and built by the Longs in 1987, Griffin Court has a traditional French brick exterior. The years they lived in New Orleans, when Noah attended Tulane University and Marilyn, Sophie Newcomb College, deepened their appreciation for New Orleans lifestyle, and the Longs incorporated distinctive New Orleans elements in the house's interior design and decor.

Ten-foot-high beveled glass doors open on a dramatic two-story central atrium furnished to resemble a New Orleans courtyard. From the courtyard wrought iron and brick stairs lead past a triple-tier cast iron fountain to an upper gallery. The back side of the fireplace features an inside triple gas grill with a copper hood.

The main floor also contains the living room, dining room, kitchen, master suite, office, entertainment area, pub bar, and the guest suite with its own kitchen, bath, and sitting area. The upper floor contains bedrooms with double French doors that open on to balconies overlooking the atrium.

The glass enclosed back porch, with a hot tub and spa, offers a view of the swimming pool. The room can be heated and air conditioned or, when the large sliding doors are opened, simply enjoyed as a screened porch.

This Coupon entitles the bearer to one ...

DELUXE "TRADITIONAL" NEW YEAR'S DAY BRUNCH...*

ABSOLUTELY FREE!!!!!!

Offer Valid January 1, 1989   11:30 AM Redeem at Long's Coach House and Tavern

*Offer void where prohibited.
Not valid on any other day.
One coupon per couple.
Reservations required!*

*Marilyn & Noah Long
RSVP*

*All complete including drinks and dessert.
ESTABLISHED JANUARY 1, 1974

Inspired by the courtyards of New Orleans, this three story central atrium including a gas grill and three tiered fountain is the center of activity for the house. (Right)

7

The living room opens onto the courtyard with a view through 22' high windows across the atrium to the cast iron Janney Crane Fountain.

*The Longs have been sharing New Year's Day with their
friends and neighbors for over 16 years.*

*The relaxed atmosphere and warm hospitality let guests
start their New Year on a bright shiny note.*

11

The Menu

Eggs MacMarilyn

•

Hot New Year's Mush

•

Cheese Grits

•

Blackeyed Peas, Jambalaya, Sliced Ham

•

Sweet Rolls

•

Coffee with Chickory

•

Cookie Trays and Fruit Cake

•

Milk Punch, Bloody Marys, Screwdrivers

Guests gather on the brick and wrought iron stairs leading from the patterned brick atrium to the second floor gallery.

The Spencer's cozy, rustic lodge is nestled in the woods of Sandy Springs.

Please join us
for a
Beastie Feastie
Super Bowl Sunday,
January 22, 1989
from 5 P.M. till
a winner is declared

Maidee & Jim Spencer

A "Wild Game Party" for the "wildest game of the year" is a fun relaxing time for friends of Maidee and Jim Spencer to drop in and enjoy the Super Bowl. Each year's menu, chosen from a variety of delicious dishes, reflects the "hunter's bag" for that year.

Snacks and drinks are provided from kick-off until half time, when the "Beastie Feastie" begins with all kinds of wonderful, unusual treats. Because of the large number of dishes presented, guests can go through the line and come back thirty minutes later to find an entirely different meal.

The Spencers set up five televisions around the house for football viewing, including a large screen model in the trophy room. They tried organizing assorted games for non-football fans, but found everyone was having too much fun chatting to play.

This cozy, rustic lodge nestled back in the woods in the Sandy Springs area of Atlanta is the home of Maidee and Jim Spencer. Constructed on the site of a stagecoach stop for passengers travelling from Marthasville (Atlanta's name before 1836) on the Kennesaw Run, the home has an interesting history.

What is now the living room was built as a log cabin by the Boy Scouts of America in their founding year, 1910. It later was used as a hunting lodge, a school, and a country house.

The Spencers have added two more old buildings to the property. A white oak log cabin built 125 years ago in Tennessee was reconstructed as the master bedroom, and a cedar smokehouse moved from Kingstree, South Carolina is the trophy room and den. It's filled with trophies from the Spencers' wild game hunting all over the world.

The modern, two-story open kitchen has heart pine paneling from a building once located in the original Underground Atlanta. Added in 1987, it has a view of the pool and stables.

The Spencers have carefully maintained the rustic atmosphere and charm of this one-time country retreat.

14

The first building in the Spencer home is the original log cabin built by Boy Scouts in 1910 and now used as the living room.

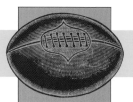

15

The Spencers designed their new two story kitchen for entertaining large groups by including a commercial stove, lots of preparation space, and a roomy eating area.

MENU

Venison Chili

Sausage Venison Cheese Dip

Roast Goose in Bourbon

Baked Pheasant in Sour Cream

Venison Pistou

Antelope or Venison Tenderloin

Ambrosia, Chocolate Moose Cake

Bronzed Quail

Caesar Salad, Wild Rice

Cranberry Waldorf Salad

Sherried Fruit Salad

Poppy Seed Bread

The "Hunter's Bag" produces a memorable beastie feastie of unusual, unexpected, tasty dishes.

The den was an old Cedar Tobacco Smoke House brought from South Carolina.

The center of activity for true football fans is the den with a big screen TV for Super—superbowl watching.

The Board of the Circle for Tallulah Falls School holds four luncheon meetings each year. The Board Meeting Committee, one of the Circle's standing committees, organizes the luncheon and coordinates the menu. Board members bring the food.

For this winter meeting hosted by Kerry Gill, committee members Suzanne Hair, Karen Mayberry, and Rita Robb served coffee and wassail at 10:00 a.m. to the fifty women attending. The meeting, which started at 10:30, was held in the basement, so the committee members could set up the luncheon, which was served upstairs.

In keeping with custom, the committee brings everything—plates, cups, coffeemaker, flatware—and cleans up afterwards. The Circle president provided a floral centerpiece as a thank you to the hostess.

This traditional brick house in the south Sandy Springs area of Atlanta is a very special home. Kerry and Andy Gill both grew up in military families, so part of what they remember from childhood is moving every couple of years.

THE CIRCLE FOR TALLULAH FALLS SCHOOL

*Winter Board Luncheon
At The Home Of Kerry Gill*

RSVP

Later, corporate transfers relocated them five times in seven years, so they had never been able to decorate a house the way they wanted.

This three-story, five bedroom house overlooking a lake was built in 1984 by Hap Schultz, who lives next door. There's plenty of room for displaying all of the family collections. The kitchen and breakfast area are open to the den and fireplace, combining elegance with warmth and welcome. Also located on the main floor is the master suite.

Kerry and Andy enjoy the wonderful full basement for entertaining, where there's a bar, full size pool table, computer room, guest room, and bath. They've filled this house with color, personality, and flair and it's where they hope to stay.

19

The Gill's brick home with a cobblestone entry court creates a welcome atmosphere.

Yellow and sunlight are synonymous with the happiness and free spirit of the Gill's home.

Everyone in the family collects things (right), so there is plenty of space planned for display such as this group of Kerry's Lladros.

In this home, the Gills were able to decorate with all the color and flair they desired.

Members of the Board take turns sharing their favorite recipes at luncheons.

After the meeting members have some time to catch up with each other, business and social.

THE M<u>E</u>N<u>U</u>

PASTISIO

□

CONGEALED ORANGE CARROT SALAD

□

CONGEALED LIME PINEAPPLE SALAD

□

TOSSED SALAD

□

FROSTED APRICOT SALAD

□

BRAN MUFFINS

□

BUTTER PECAN TURTLES

□

BROWNIES, CARAMEL BARS

□

ASSORTED FRUIT TARTS

The Winter Board Meeting of The Circle for Tallulah Falls School.

24

Carolyn Lee Wills and Rhonda Milner played matchmakers for Diane Clary (a radiologist who practices with Rhonda) and Chris Jensen (an attorney who practices with Carolyn's husband, Charles). So it was only natural that Carolyn and Rhonda, who are first cousins, would host a baby shower in anticipation of the birth of Nicholas Christian Jensen.

Carolyn, principal of Carolyn Lee Wills & Assoc. Inc., a public relations and promotions firm, planned the party. She created invitations for the shower using ultrasound pictures of Baby Nicholas, mounted on blue cards. Rhonda parked the antique wicker pram, used by her three children, in the foyer. As they entered, guests placed their shower gifts in the pram, which was rolled into the family room when it came time to open the gifts.

At the luncheon table, blue-edged placecards

Originally interested in restoring an older home, the Milners opted instead to build a new one which incorporated materials from historic sites and buildings.

were decorated with tiny baby bottles, and rocking-horse ornaments were used as napkin holders and party favors. A doll-sized wicker baby carriage served as a bread basket. The luncheon was catered by Nancy Hoffman, and Barb Griffies added her flair to the decorations, both are Circle members.

The centerpiece was a miniature table and chairs where stuffed animals wearing party hats and baby bracelets took tea from a tiny silver tea service and hand-painted china. The centerpiece was loaned by Barbara Tregellas, another Circle member, who displays the charming fantasy-provoking creatures and furniture year round, changing the table setting and costumes to reflect the seasons and holidays.

The gracious Georgian style house of Rhonda and Gene Milner sits high on a hill in the Buckhead area of Northside Atlanta, bathed in warmth and light and filled with the laughter of the Milners' three children: Kathryn, Whitner, and Cason.

Originally interested in restoring an older home, the Milners opted instead to build a new one. Completed in 1988, the house has six fireplaces and eleven foot ceilings. Many of the materials which were used in the construction of the house were salvaged from vintage buildings slated for demolition. The brick floors in the kitchen are old St. Joe brick. The exposed beams in the high-ceilinged kitchen were rescued from a building in the original Underground Atlanta. The wood and leaded-glass transom and sidelights around the front door are from a home in Virginia.

Custom millwork, including cherry paneling in the library and solid mahogany doors, was used throughout the house. Specially designed niches in the dining room walls display Rhonda's eighteenth century blue and white Chinese porcelain.

Shower gifts are displayed in a wicker baby carriage (left) which the Milners used for their three children.

Norman Askins, architect, helped the Milners design their home with eleven foot ceilings and heart of pine floors.

Croissants are served from a miniature baby stroller (left) flanked by stuffed animals dressed for the occasion.

After lunch guests gather in the family room to open presents and enjoy each other's company. Left to Right: Marilyn Cheatham, Colleen Duffy, Melissa Stanz, Lillian Braswell, Sherell White, Dr. Marjorie Homlar, Dr. Rhonda Milner, Carolyn Lee Wills, Dr. Diane Jensen, Maureen Davis, and Dianne Jaworski.

The Milner's modern kitchen has antique details such as the St. Joe brick floors and beams from old Undergound Atlanta.

THE MENU

BAKED BRIE WITH APRICOT AND PHYLLO DOUGH

FRUIT SALAD WITH POPPY SEED DRESSING

BOW TIE PASTA SALAD

SHREDDED CHICKEN SALAD WITH CURRIED MAYONNAISE DRESSING

DOUBLE CHOCOLATE BROWNIES WITH CARAMEL

ICE CREAM AND RASPBERRY SAUCE

The table centerpiece is a miniature table and chairs occupied by stuffed animals having a beastly feast on their tiny hand painted china and silver tea service.

The Milner's colorful dining room and custom cabinets are the backdrop for their collection of antique art and porcelain.

neighborliness, and good times that characterize this home.

After the excitement of the hunt, the Abreus retire for a special traditional family Easter dinner.

Northwind, the home of Lizanne and Peter Abreu, is nestled in 45 acres of rolling Roswell countryside. Designed by Peter's cousin Henri Jova, and built by Charles Black in 1974, it was situated on the site of the small A-frame structure Peter built as a young man and used when he visited the country.

Northwind's sand-hued stucco exterior has softened and mellowed with time, aided by the growth of broad-leafed Boston ivy. Weathered cedar shakes cover the roof, adding to the overall harmony of color and design. Inside, the 20-room house is a showcase for museum-quality antiques collected by the Abreu family. The living room contains a Louis XIV sofa covered in Scalamandre silk damask and a Louis Philippe lamp table. Suspended from the high ceiling is a Louis XV bronze chandelier, which hangs over a contemporary coffee table and an 18th century Savonnerie rug.

The dining room contains matching Chinese style Chippendale breakfronts and chairs from a set of 16, eight of which are presently thought to be in Windsor Castle.

As part of the Easter celebration, the Abreu family members exchange rabbits each year which become part of the decorations for the annual egg hunt.

31

The Abreu Easter Egg Hunt, begun in 1973, has become the highlight of Easter weekend for 150 or so children and grandchildren of the Abreu's friends.

Peter, Lizanne and helpers including their children, Michael, Claire and Katherine, hide 7,000 individually-wrapped candy eggs in the lush spring foliage. The family's collection of bunnies, arranged beside the driveway, greets guests as they approach.

With a hand-held microphone, Peter directs the hunt which is divided into children's age categories plus a special adult division. Prizes are awarded those who find the Golden Egg, the Silver Egg, and the most eggs. The enthusiasm is contagious as laughing children dressed in their Easter best dash in every direction.

For the adults, iced tubs of soft drinks and beer and trays mounded with cookies provide refreshment and add to the spirit of informality,

Eggstraordinary Egg Hunt

Easter Sunday, March 26, 1989
The Hunt begins at three o'clock

Peter and Lizanne Abreu
Michael, Claire & Katherine

B.Y.O. Basket   R.S.V.P.

The muted, sand-hued stucco walls covered with broad leaf Boston ivey and the weathered cedar shake roof of the Abreu home blend into the rolling hills of the 45 acre estate in Roswell. (right)

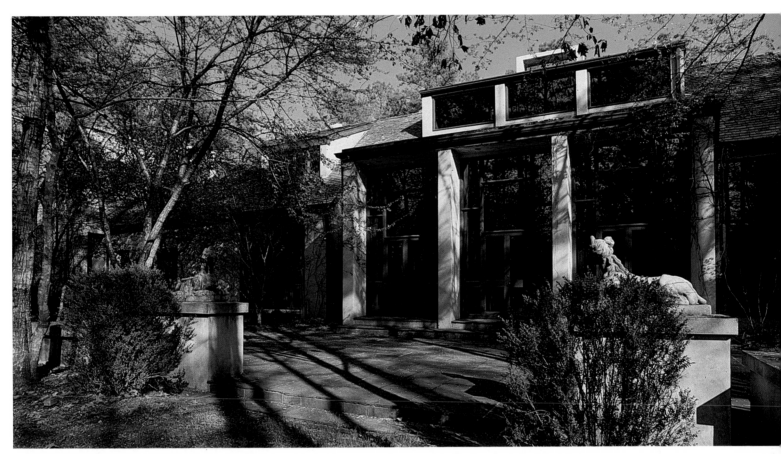

The Twin sphinxes guarding the back terrace of the Abreu home come from the old family home on Sea Island.

Jennie and Beth Harned carrying Easter baskets (left above) and dressed in their Easter best approach the annual hunt along a winding drive bordered by flowering cherry trees.

Host Peter Abreu (left below) explains the rules of the hunt to guests before signaling the quivering mass of children to begin their enthusiastic scramble for 7,000 hidden eggs.

MENU

Sausage Casserole

•

Leg of Lamb

•

Sauce Nicoise

•

Wild Rice Casserole

•

Parsley-Garlic Potatoes

•

Steamed Asparagus with Hollandaise

•

Croissants

•

Carrot Cake, Coffee

In the living room of Northwind a Louis XV Bronze chandelier hangs over an 18th century Savonnerie rug and a Louis XVI sofa covered in scalamandre silk damask.

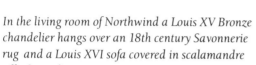

This was the first year in all fifteen years of the Annual Easter Egg hunt that the Cherry trees have actually bloomed at Easter.

The table is all set and waiting for the Abreu family's Easter dinner following the great hunt.

The bar mitzvah of Roger Adam Samuels and Robert Franklin Samuels, the sons of Cynthia and Ivan Samuels, lasted for a matter of hours but preparations began years in advance and its implications continue for a lifetime. The celebrations that followed the ceremony at Temple Emanuel recognized the new responsibilities assumed by the young men and celebrated the importance and continuity of family.

Immediately following the ceremony, friends and family returned to the Samuels' home for a special garden luncheon. The 50 guests, many from out of town, served themselves this traditional meatless meal from an attractive buffet, and found seats at tables around the patio or under a yellow and white striped canopy in the back yard.

That evening 130 guests, including many teenagers, gathered at Temple Emanuel for dinner. Before the meal, during a special ceremony, Roger and Robert lit candles and read messages of affection and thanks they had written in

Before dinner on the evening of the bar mitzvah, individuals who have played a special role in the lives of Roger and Robert were honored by a special message read to the audience and a candle lighted in their honor.

honor of friends and family members.

The bar mitzvahs are permitted to choose a theme for the dinner; Robert and Roger chose "Wheels, Wheels, Wheels" because the whole family loves automobiles. The table decorations featured model cars from the family's collection as centerpieces and theme posters were placed around the room. Guests discovered their table assignments by selecting a set of ignition keys from a board near the entrance to the dining room. Following dinner, dancing included the traditional Horah.

The two-story French Regency home of Cynthia and Ivan Samuels sits atop a wooded knoll in the Dunwoody area of Atlanta. At the front of the house, a dramatic two-story foyer contains a perfectly proportioned, double half-spiral staircase rising above an Italian marble floor.

The classic style of the house provides a dramatic backdrop for contemporary furnishings, accented with selected antique pieces such as a vintage wet bar in the den. The dining room's soft marbleized paper and heavy moldings are a pleasing background for the original sunburst design of the dining room table and the art deco black-laquered chairs.

38

ROBERT AND ROGER

OUR WORLD REFLECTS A RICH TRADITION OF YESTERDAY AND THE BRIGHT PROMISE OF TOMORROW AS WE INVITE YOU TO SHARE IN THE B'NAI MITZVAH OF OUR SONS
ROGER ADAM
AND
ROBERT FRANKLIN
ON SATURDAY, THE FIRST OF APRIL NINETEEN HUNDRED AND EIGHTY-NINE AT TEN O'CLOCK IN THE MORNING

OUR CELEBRATION CONTINUES SATURDAY EVENING AT SEVEN

CYNTHIA AND IVAN SAMUELS

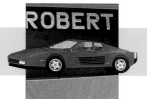

39

The sweeping lines of the front staircase (above) lead down to the imported Italian marble floor of the entry foyer.

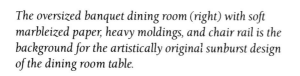

The oversized banquet dining room (right) with soft marbleized paper, heavy moldings, and chair rail is the background for the artistically original sunburst design of the dining room table.

When the boys saw the money tree of $2.00 bills given by Cynthia's tennis team, they wanted to know if they fertilized it, would it grow $20'ies?

Selected by the 13 year old boys, the theme of the evening, "Wheels, Wheels, Wheels" (below) was conveyed effectively by table centerpieces assembled from the Samuels' model cars. Decorations were done by Sally Sacha, a Circle member.

40

41

Following the ceremony, out of town guests, family, and close friends joined the Samuels in a traditional non-meat luncheon.

The Lahvosh Vegetarian Sandwiches are a healthy and easy way to make finger food. Cynthia and her friend Kathy Wentz cooked for the luncheon meal choosing a menu that could be prepared several days ahead.

MENU

LUNCHEON

BAGELS, CREAM CHEESE & NOVA SCOTIA SALMON

BAKED STUFFED BRIE

MARINATED VEGETABLES

LAHVOSH VEGETARIAN SANDWICHES

SOUR CREAM POUND CAKES

CHOCOLATE CHIP COOKIES

EGG SALAD

MELON BALLS

PASTA SALAD PRIMAVERA

SOUTHERN DEVILED EGGS

PEPSI COLA CAKES

ASSORTED COOKIES TRAYS

RECEPTION

STUFFED CABBAGE, SWEET KUGEL

CHICKEN PICCATA WITH RICE PILAF, FRESH FRUIT DISPLAY, RAW VEGETABLE BASKET

TEMPURA FRIED VEGETABLES, POTATO LATKES

SPINACH STUFFED MUSHROOMS

HAWAIIAN CHICKEN KABOBS

FRANKS IN A BLANKET

DINNER

LEMON RASPBERRY SORBET

TOSSED SALAD WITH PRESTIGE DRESSING

PRIMED RIBEYE OF BEEF

CHICKEN BREAST CONTINENTAL

ASPARAGUS HOLLANDAISE

GLAZED BABY CARROTS, LITTLE BROWN POTATOES

VIENNESE DESSERT TABLE, BUILD-YOUR-OWN-SUNDAE

OLD ENGLISH TRIFLE

CHOCOLATE COCONUT LAYER CAKE

CHOCOLATE MOUSSE WITH WHIPPED CREAM

FRUIT LAYER CAKE

IRISH COFFEE

The party was extended into the garden when lunch was served under the yellow and white striped canopy.

The Circle for Tallulah Falls School has held an annual scholarship ball for most of its 62 years. Following Atlanta custom, ball chairman Lynn Wright and auction chairman Peggy Fulghum hosted a party at the home of Nancy and Randy Rizor to thank volunteers who helped with the charity event. Lynn and Peggy did all the food preparation and cooking for about 50 people.

Guests were drawn through the house and out to the back deck by the beautiful spring weather and the lovely view of the Chattahoochee River that flows just beyond the gardens. One of the

ball centerpieces, a pot of gold, gold coins, rainbows, and colorful balloons, added a bright reminder of the successful evening for which volunteers were being honored.

This elegant and welcoming home of Nancy and Randy Rizor sits beside the Chattahoochee River in east Cobb County. The brick structure is a copy of the George Wythe house built in 1790 in Williamsburg, Virginia, described as "a brick mansion (which) represents an engaging (American) version of the English Georgian style." The feeling of authenticity is enhanced throughout the house by antiques and reproductions of period furniture in combination with custom moldings, cabinets, and mantels.

Outside, the Williamsburg-style gardens continue the colonial American theme, reflecting 17th and 18th century England. Gravel paths edged with brick join well-tended beds of roses and azaleas and manicured hedges.

For the Rizors, who maintain ten polo ponies, the proximity of their home to the Atlanta Polo Fields was a significant attraction. The entire family participates in the sport from March until the end of November. Many trophies and collected polo memorabilia decorate the house.

43

The Rizor's Williamsburg brick home is on the banks of the Chattahoochee river near the polo fields in Cobb County.

The hosts and hostesses of the Thank You Party were left to right: Dan Wright and Lynn Wright, Nancy Rizor, and Peggy and Tom Fulgham. Dr. Randy Rizor was out of town.

Lynn and Peggy prepared all the food (above) for this
party to say "Thank You" to the volunteers for the ball.

Merrilyn and Harry Burke pour punch to toast RTM
Ball sponsors Linda and Joe Gondolfo (right) joined by
Circle President, Liz Sudderth, and Noah Long.

The unique combination of flowers and fruit bring out the colors of the rainbow that were the theme for the ball.

The formal English gardens between the back of the house and the Chattahoochee river include rose trees, gravel paths, brick edging, and manicured hedges.

T · H · E · M · E · N · U

CHAMPAGNE PUNCH	BARBECUED WATER CHESTNUTS
FULL BAR	APRICOT BRIE IN PASTRY
BEEF TENDERLOIN	ARTICHOKE RICE SALAD
CHEESE PUFFS	RAW VEGGIE DIP
EMPANADITAS, CAVIAR PIE	BOURBON BROWNIES, EDITORS REQUEST

The guests were drawn out onto the rear deck by the lure of the marvelous spring weather.

The pot of gold and the rainbow centerpiece (left) for the ball tables was designed by Sally Sacha.

Dr. Shumake looks over the scrapbook filled with memories of his years with each Circle President.

ThIs sparkling Sunday evening supper was given as a loving tribute by the former presidents of the Circle to honor Dr. Franklin Shumake upon his retirement after 18 years as President of Tallulah Falls School. Martha Dinos and Jeanne Berry did most of the cooking but all of the presidents contributed to the party. Jann Kern recycled topiary tree bases used several weeks earlier for the "Pedigreed Affair" of the Atlanta Humane Society and added fresh flowers to make centerpieces for individual tables. In this way, one charity helps another; the giving overlaps!

Memories of the past 18 years were shared during cocktail hour, followed by a beautiful buffet dinner with individually preset tables in the foyer. After-dinner tributes with champagne toasts included reminiscences from each president. Dr. Shumake was presented with an engraved silver box and a scrapbook of memorabilia from the years he served. The evening honored the man who carried the school to great heights and cemented a bond with women who worked hard to make that progress reality.

This magnificent estate just inside the perimeter highway in Northwest Atlanta is the home of Martha and Anthony Dinos. Its intricate brick patterns and cedar shake roof capture the romance of provincial France and combine traditional European elegance with the ultimate in contemporary living. The original house on the property, over 50 years old, was greatly expanded in the late seventies with the addition of a new living room, kitchen, entry, and master bedroom by Martin Associates Architects.

The impressive entrance with five pairs of French doors leads to a gallery-foyer. Rich oak beams contrast with the high white stucco ceilings throughout the formal rooms and a carved French country style mantel is the focal point of the living room. The dining room chandelier hangs from crossbeams under a skylight that's centered over the glass dining table. The house is filled with antiques Martha collects as well as her assortment of ceramic cats from all over the world.

The bar built between the dining room and living room plus the large kitchen help make entertaining easy and relaxed. A cypress deck on the rear of the house overlooks a pool and a lake. This is a multi-family estate; Anthony's mother lives in the guest house and Martha's father lives in an apartment downstairs.

50

*JOIN US FOR A
SUNDAY EVENING
SUPPER
HONORING
DR. FRANKLIN SHUMAKE*

*A Loving Tribute
By Past Presidents Of
The Circle For
Tallulah Falls School*

51

MENU
CHICKEN-SHRIMP CASSEROLE

RICE PILAF

FRESH ASPARAGUS WITH HOLLANDAISE

PARKERHOUSE ROLLS

ROMAINE

RED ONIONS AND MANDARIN ORANGE SALAD
WITH POPPY SEED DRESSING

ALMOND AMARETTO CHEESECAKE

ALMOND TORTE

CHAMPAGNE FRAMBOISE

WINE WITH DINNER

The topiary trees (left above) were used earlier at the Pedigreed Affair of the Altanta Humane Society and redecorated by Jann Kern with fresh spring azaleas.

The hostesses for this retirement salute were past Presidents who served during Dr. Shumake's tenure. Seated left to right: Phyllis Haislip, Martha Dinos, Margaret Young, Jann Kern, Betty Bull, and Jeanne Berry. Standing left to right: Barbara Tregellas, Margaret Blackstock, Joan Fuller, Dr. Shumake, Brenda Tustian, Liz Sudderth, Minnie Bowden, Maidee Spencer, Carolyn Lee Wills, and Martha Gorman.

The individual dinner tables filled the entry foyer during the party (left).

Spring came right to the table with this centerpiece using bedding plants from the nursery artfully arranged in a large basket. The flamingos are hand carved and signed.

A French country style carved mantel (left) is a focal point of the living room.

After all the working lunches Dr. Shumake has shared with these ladies, he's finally partaking just for fun. (below).

On a glorious spring day, Kathleen Day and Bruce Gunter welcomed friends and family to their new purple Victorian home for a House Warming and Blessing. Guests received invitations featuring a pen and ink rendering of the house. A bountiful feast was catered by Dorothy Haynes and J. Mitchell Bowling.

As the Rev. Patricia Merchant of St. Luke's Episcopal Church conducted the house blessing service, the late afternoon sun was shining on the gathering through the stained glass window in the family room. The house literally bubbled with laughter and joy while neighbors and family enjoyed a cool May evening.

Reverend Patricia Merchant officially blessed the house.

Kathleen Day and Bruce Gunter's home on Waddell Street in Atlanta's Inman Park neighborhood combines grand turn-of-the-century style with modern convenience. Kathie's construction company, Kathleen Day & Associates, built the house on one of the seven lots Kathie purchased near the old Atlanta Stove Works factory with the idea of building new, modern houses whose floor plans and exteriors would harmonize with the neighborhood's vintage architecture.

Kathie and husband Bruce designed the four-level floor plan with the help of their neighbor, architect Richard Dagenhart, after their family outgrew the smaller house just two doors away.

The front part of the main floor is based on the Victorian four-square plan, with four rooms of equal size. A striking stained glass window by Palmer-Pohlmann studio is a collage of Atlanta landmarks that are special to Kathie and Bruce: the Fox Theater, the Georgia Tech Tower, St. Luke's Episcopal Church, the Varsity Drive-In restaurant, Zoo Atlanta, the IBM building, Coca-Cola and more.

Family bedrooms fill the second floor. In the window above the whirlpool tub in the master bath, an etched glass panel displays Inman Park's neighborhood symbol, a butterfly with two faces in its wings. One face looks to the future; the other looks to the past. Award-winning designer Virginia White added her professional touch to the interiors.

The top floor houses playrooms—one for children, one for adults—and storage. More storage space and the garage are located on the ground level.

Kathleen and Bruce built their Victorian style home (right) on the far west border of Inman Park to blend with the historic Victorian neighborhood.

The living room captures the true Victorian flavor of Inman Park in design and decoration.

This etched butterfly window features the symbol of the Inman Park Restoration. The Butterfly is the symbol of rebirth and the two faces of Inman Park honoring its past and its future.

Everyone enjoyed the spectacular fare from the oldest to the youngest, including this true affectionado of the silk swann.

The stained glass window created by Palmer-Pohlmann Studio is a collage of the Atlanta architecture and symbols Kathie and Bruce like best.

MENU

HORS D'OEUVRES
TO BE PASSED AS GUESTS ARRIVE

Goat Cheese & Spinach Baguettes

Hot Southern Cheese Puffs

**Artichoke Hearts
Wrapped in Bacon**

Pepperoni Stuffed Mushroom Caps

**Sparkling Catawba
with
Strawberries
(Non-Alcohlic)**

DINING ROOM BUFFET

**Decorated Party Sandwich Loaf
with
Cream Cheese Frosting**

**Canapes of Smoked Salmon Roses
with
Black Caviar**

**Artichoke Bottoms
Filled with
Tarragon Seafood Salad**

**Canapes of Smoked Duck Breast
with
Kiwi and Chutney**

Cheese Straws

**Linzer Cookies, Lemon Canapes, Meringue Cookies,
Cream Puff Swans, Rum Balls, Chocolate Canapes,
Butterfly Petit Fours**

Salted Pecans

Tea

Lemon Pineapple Punch

Friends and neighbors flocked to join Kathie and Bruce on their happy day.

The caterers, Dorothy Haynes and J. Mitchell Bowling, even created a Victorian atmosphere with the ornate buffet.

The perfect solution to the problem of a lot of food and a
small space is to double deck the table using mirrors and
glass bricks.

The Skidmore's palatial home, built by W. Greg Howington, sits atop the highest of the north Atlanta ridges in the foothills of the Smoky Mountains.

Franklyn and Rodger Skidmore, members of the Friends of Vieilles Maisons Francaises, hosted a musical tribute to the French bicentennial. The gathering also celebrated the restoration of a stained glass window made possible by the Atlanta Chapter of FVMF. Its goal, like that of its parent organization in France is preserving France's architectural heritage.

The guests' arrival coincided with a springtime shower, and a dramatic cloud-darkened sky provided a perfect backdrop for the program of French music. Franklyn Noll Skidmore, soprano, has delighted opera, oratorio, and orchestral audiences throughout the United States and Europe. On this evening, pianist Helen McCorkle Finch accompanied Franklyn in performances of period pieces from the time of the French Revolution and contemporary classics by French composers. They were joined by Lee Heuerman on flute for some selections. Tristan Foison, a French composer and conductor living in Atlanta, performed a work dedicated to him by the composer Messaien.

Fresh spring flowers were placed in the entrance hall and living and dining rooms by Catherine Walther of Arrangements. Her sprays of tea roses, draped around the arms of the dining room chandelier, seemed inspired by notes from a musical score. Following the program, the guests sampled delicious treats and enjoyed the cool evening atmosphere around the pool.

On Atlanta's northwestern rim, the home of Franklyn and Rodger Skidmore sits atop the highest ridge, commanding a majestic view. The Skidmores moved here in 1987 with their children Andrew and Chamblis, after spending 18 months building this French manor house.

The 24-foot high glass bay at one end of the living room cradles a grand piano and provides a setting for the Skidmores' frequent musicals. The space was designed to maximize the grand multi-directional view and to project vocal and instrumental tones with brilliance and clarity.

The living room mantel has a 12 foot, garland-draped trumeau and side panel with musical motif decorations that mask cabinets which contain stereo speakers and Franklyn's music scores. The mantel, the pilasters framing the living room windows, and the raised panels under the dining room chair rail were executed by Kenneth McDonald of the Mantel Market. Nearby, the media room houses controls for seven sound systems and storage for tapes, records, and compact discs.

Outside, a multi-level terrace surrounds a pool and planted areas that landscape architect Henry Schutte adapted from the design of the reflecting pools at Chateaux Vaux Le Viscount just south of Paris.

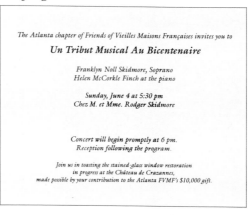

The musical tribute to the French Bicentennial (right) was dedicated to the memory of Carol Barrett Longchampt, founder of the local chapter of FVMF.

Following the musical tribute, Franklyn and her fellow
performers left to right Tristan Foison, Franklyn, Helen
McCorkle and Lee Heuerman, enjoyed compliments by
the pool.

The 24 foot high glass bay at the end of the living room
not only facilitates one's enjoyment of the multi-
directional vista but projects vocal and instrumental
tones with brilliance and clarity during frequent
musicals.

The back of the house overlooks a pool and planted area designed as an adaptation of the reflecting pools at Chateaux Vaux Le Viscount just south of Paris.

Catherine Walther's simple but elegant summer floral arrangements (right) graced the entry foyer.

The majestic living room mantel and grand pilasters framing the living room windows were done by Kenneth McDonald of the Mantel Market.

MENU

☐ ☐ ☐

White Wine

☐ ☐ ☐

Smoked Salmon Spread
with
Caviar Toast Points

☐ ☐ ☐

Baked Brie in Puff Pastry
with
Apricots and Pecans

☐ ☐ ☐

Fresh Seasonal Fruit Tray
with
Amaretto Dipping Sauce

☐ ☐ ☐

Liver Pate
with
Pistachio Nuts
and
Cognac

☐ ☐ ☐

Fresh Asparagus
with
Tarragon Cream

☐ ☐ ☐

66

The magnificent explosion of summer garden flowers cascaded from ceiling to table reflecting the romantic flair of Catherine Walther of Arrangements.

Among the guests (below) were, left to right, Mary Beth Garrecht, Roger Skidmore, Franklyn Skidmore, Florence Cloudt, Pat Williams, Margot Houchins, Susan Tucker and Homer A. Houchins. Chateau Elan provided all the wine for the evening.

A swann filled with Queen Anne's Lace was the fanciful symbol for this enchanted evening.

Elizabeth and Carl Allen's party was an enchanted evening, capturing the spirit of days of yore. Elizabeth's eye for detail was evident in the careful planning and coordination of the decor, food, and entertainment.

Randy Cotton of Atlanta Floral Arts spun his magic around the pool and throughout the house, where huge English urns cascaded with soft pink peonies and other summer garden flowers. Guests lingered inside where drinks were served or strolled out beside the pool where baroque tunes were played on a harpsicord and the smell of gardenias and roses wafted through the air. Poolside, a giant swan was filled with Queen Anne's Lace picked from the Allens' wildflower meadow.

Eight tables were draped in custom-made cloths that echoed the house's color scheme. Each table displayed a different centerpiece, and each was set with different antique china, silver, and crystal. Elizabeth has collected much of this through the years from the estate sales department of Maier and Berkele Jewelers. A formal, seated seven-course dinner was prepared and served by Lee Epting caterers.

Guests were entertained during dinner by a costumed court jester, who juggled and quipped as he moved from table to table on a unicycle.

Trifles, Truffles and other English desserts were served from the heavily laden buffet in the dining room.

In a quiet bend of the Chattahoochee River north of Atlanta sits O' Sole Mio, the 13 acre estate of Elizabeth and Carl Allen. The Allens' desire to be close to nature drew them to the property, which they bought five years ago when they moved here from Dallas, Texas.

The house's English country design is strongly influenced by the architecture of Normandy. Graceful, tall bay windows soften the effect of the hard-laid stone exterior. The Allens have been told two stories about the origin of the stone: one story says it came from a Georgia county courthouse that was demolished; the other traces the stone's origin to cobblestones from downtown Atlanta's streets.

Beautiful antiques combine with comfortable furniture to make this a house the family can relax in and enjoy. Most of the decorating work had been done by Jeannie Bazer of Dallas; Pat Birdsall, a Circle member, in Atlanta has helped since the move.

The front door opens into a two-story round entry hall. To the left is a library and office Elizabeth uses, panelled in Missouri black walnut. Beyond the library is a master bedroom suite with a formal sitting area and fireplace. The bedroom opens out to the pool. The living room holds the Allens' ivory collection started by Carl's great grandfather, who brought a chess set back from China.

The entire estate has been beautifully landscaped, without being "hard-edged," giving the impression that the hand of man has touched these acres most gently.

During dinner the guests were entertained by a roving court jester.

The Allen's home, O' Sole Mio, is an English country estate in the midst of 13 acres along the Chattahoochee river in Sandy Springs.

A Midsummer's Evening

Elizabeth and Carl Allen request the pleasure of your company for cocktails and dinner Friday, June 9, 1989 7:30 p.m.

RSVP - Diana Brannon

The den overlooking the pool is a favorite gathering place for the Allen family.

This dessert buffet, fit for a king, is equally as delicious as it is beautiful.

The Allens wake up each morning to the reflection of the rising sun on the pool just outside their bedroom doors.

This cozy, paneled library is Elizabeth's office for planning charity events as well as home entertaining.

71

Randy Cotton of Atlanta Floral Arts made each table an individual artistic display with different flower arrangements, place settings, and antique decorative pieces.

MENU

PEROSHKIS	NEW POTATOES ROSEMARY
KNISHES	ANGEL BISCUITS
SMOKED TROUT FILET	CHEESECAKE ROGET
CROUTONS, SALAD OF SWEET LETTUCES	CELEBRATION LOAF
RASPBERRY VINIAGRETTE DRESSING	OLD ENGLISH TRIFLE
FILET OF BEEF BEARNAISE	CHOCOLATE STRAWBERRY GRAND MARNIER
ASPARAGUS WITH LEMON BUTTER	CHOCOLATE TRUFFLES
BAKED TOMATO	CHOCOLATE RUM VACHERIN

The old English Court music combined with the fragrance of gardenias and roses in Randy Cotton's floral arrangements transported guests to the days of yore.

The guests at each table were served on a different antique china pattern. Much of the antique silver and china came from Atlanta's oldest jeweler, Maier and Berkele.

The emerald green formal garden of Bettye and Tom Lowe's home on Atlanta's West Paces Ferry Road was the perfect setting for their daughter Kathryn's wedding reception.

Kathryn's husband, Bryan Blackburn, was a fraternity brother of her oldest brother, Tim. For years, when friends asked Bryan when he would marry, he'd say he was waiting for Kathryn to grow up. Bryan is from Auburn, Alabama, and Kathryn is a graduate of Auburn University. Their wedding ceremony took place at the Cathedral of St. Philip on Peachtree Road.

The reception was catered by Affairs to Remember. Floral garlands designed by Priscilla's Potpourri drew guests through the formal foyer out on to the pillared terrace. A combo and roving bagpipe players provided atmosphere for the afternoon.

Massive quantities of edible treats were displayed in tiers repeating the theme of the gardens including fruit, foliage, flowers, and statuary.

The guest list was a long and political one; Tom is a Fulton County Commissioner, Bettye a former State Representative, and there are four children in the family. Kathryn was the Lowe's third child to have a wedding reception at the house. Bettye says her children's friends call it their "Halfway House"—halfway between where they've been and where they are going.

"Dellbrook," designed by Owen James Southwell, was built in 1929 in the Tuxedo Park development now known as Buckhead. Fifteen years ago, the house and its contents had come up for public auction. Bettye and Tom Lowe attended the auction to bid on the pool furniture, but ended up buying the whole house.

In the James River tradition, Dellbrook was designed with two fronts: the road front which faces West Paces Ferry Road and the river front which faces the garden. The entry foyer is particularly spectacular, with a circular stairway over the door, mural walls, the original chandelier, and half-glass doors that open on to the

The quiet Koi pool and lush gardens designed by Edith Henderson were the ideal setting for a romantic wedding reception.

wide, pillared veranda. The living room is filled with antiques and dominated by Joseph Highmore paintings.

With help of decorator Nancy Green, the Lowes have made a comfortable liveable home for their family, emphasizing bright colors, usable antiques, and careful modernization. They converted the original servants' quarters to an apartment for their son; then it became Bettye's office. The remodeled kitchen combined the former kitchen, butler's pantry, breakfast area, and three small pantries to create a roomy, bright, extremely functional modern space.

Edith Henderson redesigned the formal gardens for the Lowes. The Summer Garden was the scene of their son Scott's wedding and reception.

Mr. and Mrs. Thomas Marvell Lowe, Jr.
request the honour of your presence
at the marriage of their daughter
Kathryn Dell
to
Mr. Bryan Martin Blackburn, II
Saturday, the twenty-fourth of June
nineteen hundred and eighty-nine
at half after twelve o'clock
The Cathedral of Saint Philip
Atlanta, Georgia

Three of the Lowe's children have had receptions at Dellbrook.

The welcoming flavor of this original Buckhead home is captured in the grand entry foyer which opens onto the pillared back terrace. Flowers from Priscilla's Potpourri were everywhere from the doors to the cakes.

The couple was blessed with a glorious sunny day to celebrate during one of Atlanta's rainiest summers.

The Lowe's formal living room is dominated by the Joseph Highmore paintings.

The Menu

CHAMPAGNE
FRESH FRUIT DISPLAY
FRESH VEGETABLES
STUFFED MUSHROOM CAPS WITH CRABMEAT
SUN-DRIED TOMATO & MOZZARELLA TARTLETS
SLICED BAKED HAM AND TURKEY BREAST
PUNCH
CHEESE ASSORTMENT
SHRIMP PUFFS
CALIFORNIA GAZPACHO PIE
SMOKED SALMON CHEESE CAKE
WEDDING CAKES

Hoffer's Bakery created tiers of joy in these fanciful wedding cakes.

The gigantic iced fruit display with honeydew, cantaloupe, pineapple, strawberries, and grapes was a favorite on this hot summer afternoon.

The happy Bride, Groom, and guests celebrated, danced, and toasted the future on the terrace and in the formal gardens of Dellbrook.

The Morris's home in the heart of Sandy Springs is a copy of the Moot House in Savannah.

Cheri and Terry Morris picked the Fourth of July holiday for a special family celebration. They originally planned to do all the cooking and preparation themselves, but business and travel pressures demanded they get help.

Cheri, an accomplished party planner who operates a public relations firm, Morris & Fellows, located a caterer who was willing to use recipes from the family collection to prepare favorites, such as Grandma Campbell's Baked Beans. A separate agency was hired to take charge of serving.

When guests arrived at cocktail time, they were directed to a backyard table piled with magazines and instructed to use the magazines to make buttons and wear them to express their statements for the day.

Tables were set country style in the backyard, and guests served themselves at a buffet. Beautiful tabletop flower arrangements from Mark Pancerz incorporated favorite family objects, such as dolls, a trumpet, and the cigar box where Terry kept his "treasures" as a boy.

Because Cheri and Terry both attended Florida State University and were members of the famous Florida State Circus, the after-dinner entertainment centered on circus feats. Terry and son Collin juggled fire; afterward, the amazed guests were invited to try their hands at juggling. The children enjoyed getting in on the act! Then came dessert; a table of family favorites included big barrels of ice cream for topping hot helpings of Aunt Lucille's Peach Cobbler.

As night fell, the fireworks began and a dazzling display of booming fireworks echoed from all over the city. Sparklers, as always, enchanted the children.

When the host and his son juggle fire, it really lights up a party.

CAN WE SPARK YOUR INTEREST?

80

The floor plan and exterior design of Cheri and Terry Morris' three-story colonial home on a cul-de-sac in the heart of Sandy Springs replicates the Moot House in Savannah. They bought the house three years ago when it was under construction and personally supervised the finish details, color, and trim. Cheri also designed the pattern for the beveled edge glass doors and the fanlight between the living room and den.

A rose ash accent wall combines a specially hand woven rug and hand painted fireplace tiles to create a pretty pastel palette in the sunny living room. The Morris' collection of "funny" carved birds is scattered throughout the house, which is furnished with family heirlooms and antiques Cheri and Terry have acquired.

The decor of the dining room was inspired by the art deco chandelier that came from a home they once owned in Wichita, Kansas.

The large, sunny den with French doors leading to a patio is wonderful for entertaining and relaxing. The backyard, with its terraced gardens and walls, carries through with the feel of a Savannah courtyard filled with flowers.

Family dessert recipes can still make an impressive display with the right artist. Mark Pancerz did the extravagant floral arrangements throughout the house.

Family antiques (left) are beautifully set off by the brilliant color palette selected by the Morrises.

This fun family celebration of our nation's birthday had something for everyone.

Cheri and Terry Morris share dessert with Linda and Jerry France. Jerry is President of Communications Channels which prints "Business Atlanta".

When the Morris's have a family party, they have family food everyone will enjoy.

MENU

BARBECUE PORK SANDWICHES	BAKED BEANS
LAYERED SUMMER SALAD	SOUTHERN FRUIT SALAD
SOUR CREAM POUND CAKE	PEACH COBBLER
BANANA PUDDING	

Everyone's a child when the fireworks display starts.

The "funny" carved birds found in the den and around the house are a "fun" collection.

85

Marianne Broadbear, Jill Dowd, and Susan Whipple planned a birthday party for their sixteen-year-old sons, Michael, Dusty, and Harvard, respectively. As the day of the party approached, the birthday theme became a decoy for a surprise party for Dusty, who would soon be moving to Dallas. The three mothers came up with what they thought was a fun, somewhat unusual, party but their sons had a different idea. The boys all laughed politely when Marianne, whose etiquette classes they had attended since she is president of Success Image and Young Sophisticates, jokingly suggested a sit-down dinner.

The mothers' original menu was changed to incorporate the boys' favorite dishes. Michael Broadbear, Sr. is the attorney for W.D. Crowley's Restaurants, and the boys have grown up eating there. Hence, the Southern Birthday Bar-B-Q.

Jill is an artist of some note, and the decorations were gathered from her collections of Western-inspired art. The mothers created a masculine table arrangement incorporating some of Dusty's treasures for the twig table in Jill's solarium. The boys dubbed it "straight from Indiana Jones."

Jill's carousel horse was moved outside for soft drinks, minted tea, and snacks. Clear plastic glasses were used around the pool for safety. To make serving easy, red plastic plates and forks, along with party favors which were miniature collectors' cars containing fortunes, were tied up in red bandannas. The centerpieces on the wrought iron tables were red bandannas and cowboy hats.

The dress of the day was plaid shirts, jeans, and cowboy hats with the boys "toting" (in the vernacular of cowboys) funny remembrance gifts for Dusty. To maintain the birthday party hoax and keep Dusty from realizing this was his going away party, the gifts were designated with Michael, Dusty, and Harvard's names. When Lisa Gardner of Savory and Sage Catering rang a cowbell to corral the boys for dessert, the boys sang, "For He's a Jolly Good Cowpoke," and presented the gifts to Dusty.

The French country home of Jill and Doug Dowd was built around the double front doors salvaged from an eighteenth century French castle. The doors have the Napoleonic bee in the ironwork and are signed by Werner, who made them.

The whole house, inside and out, is designed to look old. With the many explicit details they wanted in this home, Doug preferred to take on the role of builder.

Jill says the most unique thing about the house is the roof, which resembles old stone and acquires more patina with each rain. The concrete tiles are graduated in size from top to bottom.

Almost every door, wall, ceiling, and floor throughout the house was handpainted by Scott Waterman. The doors in the foyer were decorated with French floral scenes and sanded to look weathered.

The pecky cypress wood ceilings and beams in the dining and living room were stained a soft turquoise, handpainted with flowers, and blotted to give an aged look. To achieve the same effect the walls were striated vertically and horizontally with a broom.

New meets old in the kitchen and breakfast area, where the ceiling was painted to look water spotted and wall-to-wall wood cabinets were distressed and antiqued in a soft turquoise. An avid cook, Jill is especially fond of her gas restaurant range with its pilot light she uses to make her homemade bread rise. The floors are flagstone, easy to keep and great for pool access.

This home is filled with Jill's paintings and collections.

The Battle for the greased watermelon was one of many contest games played in the pool.

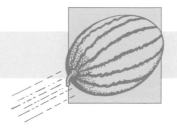

The Dowd's built their home around these exquisite eighteenth century doors from a castle in France.

In the living room the fireplace has been painted to resemble three different colors of marble while the pecky cypress wood ceilings and beams have been stained a soft turquoise, handpainted with flowers and blotted to give an old look.

The Solarium also serves as a gallery for some of Jill Dowd's paintings.

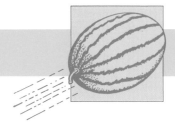

89

Tiffany Dowd serves hors d'oeuvres to the birthday boys and their guests from the antique carousel horse.

A meal in this cozy breakfast nook is like a trip back in time.

MENU

Crowley's BBQ Ribs
Parmesan Pita Bread
Watermelon Whale
Garlic Bread
Four Way Chocolate Cake
Red Beans & Rice
Deviled Eggs
Fresh Vegetable Tray
Cokes
Cole Slaw
Pumpkin Torte

*The adults favorite was the pumpkin torte done by Lisa
Gardner of Savory and Sage Caterers. Left to right are:
Doug Dowd, Jill Dowd, Harvard Whipple, Susan Whip-
ple, Brian Pouemer, Lisa Gardner, Mike Broadbear, and
Marianne Broadbear.*

The children and grandchildren of Kitty and Guy Lites planned a gala 50th wedding anniversary celebration that began with a reception for family members and close friends at the home of their son and daughter-in-law, Cindy and Eddie Lites.

The home was decorated with bouquets of exotic flowers. Gold bows were everywhere, reminding guests that this was the golden anniversary of the day Kitty and Guy tied the knot. A toast to 50 years of happiness was held in the den before going on to a larger reception for 150 guests at the Atlanta Athletic Club. Music of the couple's era was being played by an orchestra when the guests arrived for dinner.

Kitty and Guy Lites, native Atlantans, were married in 1939 in a small ceremony at his home in Buckhead. 50 years later, Kitty was excited to have the large, elaborate reception she missed as a bride. The next day, the "bride and groom" left on a second honeymoon.

Fifty years later, Kitty and Guy finally cut an elaborate wedding cake.

Cindy and Eddie Lites' new home was built in the private north Fulton County golf community, Country Club of the South. They carefully chose a lot on the highest ridge of the development to take full advantage of the view out the floor to ceiling windows across the back of the house.

The house is a combination of two floor plans designed to work together. The exterior and front part of the house are traditional Georgian style, with a wide-columned front porch. The front door opens to a center hallway flanked with equal-sized living and dining rooms. The back of the house has a more modern arrangement of open, airy rooms which flow together for entertaining ease.

Cindy Lites and Rita Robb are partners in Southern Design Associates of Atlanta, and the house is a showcase for their talent with design and color. Much of the furniture, several paintings and porcelain, was purchased in England.

91

The Children and Grandchildren of
Kitty and Guy Lites
cordially invite you to celebrate their
Fiftieth Wedding Anniversary
Sunday, the thirteenth of August
nineteen hundred and eighty-nine
at seven o'clock
Atlanta Athletic Club
Athletic Club Drive
Duluth, Georgia

*Friends and family gathered in the den to offer toasts
and best wishes to the anniversary couple.*

93

Lewis Reeves Properties built the Lites' Georgian style home atop the highest ridge in Country Club of the South.

The deep brilliant colors of the rug provide the basis for the decor of the living room. The magnificent carpets in this room and the entire home are from Persian Gallery.

This family kitchen and gathering place has everything: a keeping room with a fireplace, a breakfast area using pews as seats; and a state-of-the-art modern kitchen. McGregor Rowe Draperies made all of this come together with their special designs on windows, table, and chairs. Their talent is visible in window treatments throughout the house.

This bountiful display of tempting treats was unique with its riotous color as well as unusual combination of elements.

The **50** *Menu*

RECEPTION

Small Wedding Cake

Cornucopia of Fresh Vegetables

Portwine Cheese in Bread Rounds

Montrachet Cheese Tart

Fruit and Cheese Trays

Champagne

Coffee

DINNER PARTY

Hanging Beef with Breads and Condiments

Sliced Whole Ham

Sliced Whole Turkey

Bacon-Wrapped Scallops

Smoked Salmon

Pasta Station with Clam

Fettucine and Red Marinara Sauces

Fresh Fruit with Chocolate and Orange Sauces for dipping

Fresh Vegetables

Wedding Cake

Along with exotic flowers, fresh vegetables were added to make a breathtaking centerpiece. Port wine cheese balls were served in edible baskets of hollowed out bread loaves.

95

The celebration progressed from intimate to grand when moved from the Lites home to the Atlanta Athletic Club and a dinner for 200.

The bicentennial of the first election of the President of the United States is a wonderful time for a red, white, and blue celebration. Sally and Jack Rogers marked the occasion by giving a special thank-you dinner party for ten friends who helped them create the home of their dreams.

The election theme was carried out with flags, straw hats, and balloons, and Jack donned his Uncle Sam suit to greet guests at the door. As cocktails were served, night fell and the spectacular lights of the city below provided entertainment. To locate their places at the dinner table, guests drew the names of a President or First Lady and matched those identities with names on the placecards. Dinner in the elaborately decorated dining room was a special low-cholesterol meal catered by the Westin Peachtree Plaza Hotel. After the white-glove, formally served dinner, the guests applauded the chef and his staff.

A "home with a view" is exactly what Sally and Jack Rogers got when they bought two units high above the city in Park Place on Peachtree. The Rogers removed a wall and combined the two units to make an impressive spacious English country manor in the air. The space seems unlimited because every room has a balcony with a spectacular vista.

The abundant use of green in the decor ties the rooms to the green sea of trees below. When the pocket French doors between the living room and dining room are closed, the beveled mirrored panes reflect the city and the trees.

The hunter green library off the living room is especially welcoming with its light wood paneling and a mantel John Craft created from architectural antiques. The walls are covered in colorful fabric tapestry that features trees.

Next to the library, an office and exercise room connects to the large master suite. The kitchen and breakfast area boast cabinets with hand-

Sally and Jack Rogers' guests are always entertained with the twinkling lights of the downtown Atlanta skyline.

98

painted flowers and an eating area with white latticework, blue walls and ceiling to convey the feeling of an outdoor gazebo.

Combining the two units also allowed a private entrance for the Rogers' daughter and a way for caterers and help to have access to the kitchen without disturbing party guests. Sally and Jack love the highrise lifestyle for its convenience, safety, and the multitude of services the management provides. This home is everything the Rogers hoped it would be: warm, welcoming and happy.

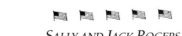

*SALLY AND JACK ROGERS
INVITE YOU TO A
BICENTENNIAL ELECTION CELEBRATION
COCKTAILS AND DINNER*

RSVP

The entrance of the modern highrise has old world charm. Each guest was greeted with a straw hat and white rose boutonniere to set the mood.

99

A living room in the sky changes it's decor as the view changes with each new season.

The hunter green library off the living room is a quiet retreat with an impressive mantel put together by John Craft using a collection of architectural antiques.

Red, White, and Blue truly carried the day with a table just bursting with patriotic pride. Such fun decorations were found at Buckhead Celebrates.

101

Each place setting was different and assembled from Sally and her mother's vast collection. Favors at each place added to the fun and formality of the settings.

The healthy, yet tasty, low cholesteral meal was catered by the Westin Peachtree Plaza Chef Makus Muller.

MENU

Rabbit Pate
Salad with Herb Vinaigrette
Stuffed Chicken Breast
Assorted Berries on Pear-Couli
Vanilla Kipfert
Anis Cookies

Seedless Black Grapes with Lemon Sherbet
Tomato-Saffron-Couli
Gourgette Nicoise
Linzer Cookies
Nero Cookies

The honored guests for this party were John Craft of John Craft Interiors and his staff. Left to Right: Jack Rogers, Sally Rogers, Norman Stone, Peggy Stone, Sandy Kasten, Sue Kasten, Rene Joel, John Craft, Chase Rogers, Benjie Tarbutton, Nancy Gandy, and Spence Gandy.

This grand and gracious home rising from the mists of the river's edge was inspired by the Louisiana Lowland style homes found along the banks of the Mississippi between New Orleans and Baton Rouge.

Thanksgiving Day at the home of Jan and Bill Collins is a very special occasion, bringing together family members from Maryland, Tennessee, Florida and all parts of Georgia. The annual reunion provides food and activities to generate those wonderful feelings of family unity and affection.

Begun many years ago at the home of Dr. Collins' mother, the tradition has continued for the past two decades at Jan and Bill's. In the early years, Jan did all the preparation and cooking herself but as the numbers grew, family members convinced her to let them help. These days, everyone contributes something to the day's feast that includes cranberry apple casserole, sweet potato souffle, and a dozen or more other picturesque and delicious dishes.

The day is filled not just with food, but with activities which bring the family together and promote a sense of continuity and tradition. An important part of the day is the 5K "Turkey Trot" held on a jogging trail close to the house. Custom made teeshirts go to anyone who runs, walks or even finishes (stroller rides qualify) the

three-mile distance. "Turkey Review," a once-a-year talent show held on a specially-constructed stage in the family room is an excellent opportunity for old-fashioned fun. Everyone, from small children to adults, dances, plays musical instruments, sings, or tells stories.

It's a terrific opportunity for the family to come together in love and thankfulness, enjoying a great meal and wonderful fellowship.

A classic southern home built in the Louisiana Lowland style, Rivermist is set on the banks of the Chattahoochee River in Atlanta. When Jan and Bill Collins built the house in 1975, they combined old with modern, antique with high tech to accommodate their family and entertaining requirements. Distinguished architect, Knox Griffin, designed Rivermist, and Gene Singleton was the builder.

The decorations and furnishings are primarily English and French antiques with oriental accents. The large rooms comfortably showcase the art and collectibles the Collins family mem-

Come Join Us For The 22rd Annual
TURKEY TROT
The Collins' Thanksgiving Family Feast
Thursday, November
Jann & Bill Collins
RSVP

bers have acquired during their travels all over the world.

The floors in the great room and hallways are from the Finnley House circa 1830 in Macon. Palladian windows in the 22 foot ceilinged great room overlook the Chattahoochee River. The library on the balcony in the room was inspired by the set of "My Fair Lady."

Upstairs, the Georgia Bulldog Room serves triple duty as a play area, an exercise room, and video center. Adjoining that is a stage area where the Collins family and their friends give live dramatic and musical performances for family members and guests. This kind of encouragement helped lead one family member, Courtney Collins, a former Miss Atlanta, to a career on the musical stage.

The beautiful grounds surrounding the home include a pool, tennis court, and wisteria arbor, and create a idyllic setting for memorable occasions.

Everyone is a winner in the annual Turkey Trot,
a three mile excursion on a joggling trail near Rivermist.

THE MENU

Roasted Turkeys and Dressing

Baked Country Ham

Fresh Smoked Ham

Cranberry Apple Casserole

Sweet Potato Souffle

Rice and Gravy, Squash Casserole

Greens Beans

Cranberry Salad

Boiled Custard, Pineapple Carrot Cake

Hot Milk Cake

Ambrosia

Chocolate Sheet Cake

On a specially constructed stage (left above) in the upstairs portion of the house, family members perform a hysterical version of "Gone with the Wind" in the annual Turkey Review.

The Collins' collection of musical angels (left) comes from all over the world.

The Collins' family circle joins hands in prayer before the annual Thanksgiving feast. The blessing is traditionally rendered by daughter, Courtney.

The first dash was made to the table and the second dash to the river (left) to run off the usual Thanksgiving over indulgence.

Orthopedic surgeon, Bill Collins, expertly carves the turkey.

Thanksgiving is the ideal occasion for all generations to share delicious family favorites.

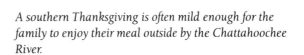

A southern Thanksgiving is often mild enough for the family to enjoy their meal outside by the Chattahoochee River.

The vivid colors and decoration of this home make the Christmas season come alive for all the Quillin's guests.

Christmas Eve dinner at RoseMary and Bill Quillin's began as a family yuletide celebration. Just after the Quillins moved to Atlanta 17 years ago, their son was chosen to play in a band at the Orange Bowl on New Year's Day. He had to leave for Miami on Christmas morning, so his parents wanted to have a Christmas Eve party he would remember.

They invited the whole family, plus neighbors and friends who invited their neighbors and friends. People who have come to the Quillins' party know they're always welcome to dinner if they're in Atlanta at Christmas. Friends of the Quillins' children who first attended the party as teenagers come back every year, bringing their children.

RoseMary always prepares for the party early. She sets the table two nights ahead, using antiques and fine china. Guests were served beautiful gourmet treats from a series of chefs until one year when a communication disaster forced a change in the menu.

Weeks before the party, RoseMary had conferred with the caterer. She thought she was placing an order for the whole dinner; he thought she was discussing her menu and ordering a centerpiece and some side dishes. Imagine her surprise when he arrived at 4:30 on Christmas Eve!

With more than 100 guests scheduled to arrive at eight o'clock, the family went into action. Bill went to work on his famous baked beans; RoseMary made tons of macaroni and cheese. They sent their son for a honeybaked ham and called the local Snack 'N' Shop deli for smoked salmon, salads, and desserts. Several friends brought additional desserts to complete the meal.

That night, dinner was a hit! Party-weary guests loved the family food on this family night. The Quillins haven't changed the menu since.

RoseMary and Bill Quillin live on an island of Tran "Quillin" ty in the heart of the bustling Buckhead area of Atlanta. Their French country house sits off the street, down a hill, and behind a wall.

The house was built with entertaining in mind. Their Christmas Eve party often has over 100 guests and

The Quillins' island of Tran-Quillin-ity sits right in the middle of bustling Buckhead.

summer parties can include even more, so the space expands to accommodate very large crowds.

One unique feature for expanded entertaining is the combination carport/gazebo with fancy wood trim and a brass chandelier built off the den near the entrance to the house. A carport in winter, the Quillins add a carpet, big plants, and tables to make a whole room that expands for outdoor summer entertaining.

The living room is two stories tall, with a library at the top of the stairs. The house contains two master suites, one upstairs and one down, plus a beautiful guest bedroom with a tented ceiling.

RoseMary, a professional model, with her sense of high style and personal flair creates a warm atmosphere that makes guests feel welcome.

Quillins' Christmas Eve Dinner

December 24, 7 til

Come if you can and bring everyone—guests & family!

111

*Even this fairyland of a guest room, complete with
tented ceiling, is decorated for Christmas.*

RoseMary collects these charming miniature houses (above) each year on her trips to Europe.

At the Quillins' even the antique bears share in the fantasy of Christmas.

Mirror, Mirror on the wall reflect the holiday season for all!

Typical of RoseMary's flair for the unusual, she had out of season long-stem white tulips flown to Atlanta for Linda Blackman's arrangement.

The fanciful centerpiece for the dessert table was done by Renee Feldman and Fran Landau of the Snack 'N' Shop Deli who also provide an assortment of delicious dishes the Quillins' serve. RoseMary's lighted miniature houses are the inspiration for the castle cakes.

MENU

CRANBERRY PUNCH	FRESH COCONUT CAKE
HONEY BAKED HAM	PINK DYNAMITE SOUFFLE
SMOKED SALMON	CHOCOLATE MOUSSE
BAKED BEANS	CHEESE CAKE
MACARONI & CHEESE	ROLLS & RYE BREAD
SHRIMP PASTA SALAD	CRANBERRY JELLO MOLD
POTATO SALAD	

IDEAS

Thanksgiving—*Get a family reunion moving after long car rides with children or a big heavy meal—a long walk or run with tee shirts as souvenirs for each year.*

Christmas Eve Dinner—*This is a very "family" night and no one wants a fancy catered meal (plus the caterer wants to be at home with his family) so put all your resources together. Gather your favorite "family" food from the deli, your family, and friends to make a meal all ages will enjoy. The more who contribute the more they share the joy!*

New Year's Day—*Nothing looks more barren than the Christmas tree with no gifts beneath it, but your tree is a big part of the decorations. Solve your gift wrapping and naked tree problems with Christmas bags. Make big and small bags with appliques for decorations. These are great wrappers for little children or large hard to wrap gifts and become part of your tradition used over and over.*

As you open the other gifts Christmas day, use the left over paper and stuffing to refill the bags as they empty and put them back under the tree. It solves a wrapping problem, a Christmas trash problem, and the naked tree! P.S. People love getting these bags as Christmas gifts!

Ladies Board Luncheon—*January tends to be cold and sterile. What can perk up a meeting and put springtime smiles on those ladies' faces? Serve a hot Wassail Punch when they arrive. Even if they drink coffee, the enticing smell will invigorate everyone who comes through the door.*

Bar Mitzvah—*Pound Cake is a family favorite but not always a spectacular cake to display. Solve that*

problem by decorating it with spring or summer flowers.

Thank You Party—*Volunteers really feel welcome when the chairmen of an event do all the cooking themselves to say more than a true Thank You! They really work to show they appreciate all the work.*

Dinner Honoring Dr. Shumake—*Buy a centerpiece from another charitable event and rework it for a dinner party. That way one charity helps another and you are ahead with your job as a hostess.*

Victorian House Blessing—*When people are invited to a house warming and tour your home, make even the bathtub special by floating flowers in it.*

Victorian House Blessing—*Short of space and expecting lots of people! Double the height of one of your tables making it two tiered. Using a mirror as a base for this arrangement and a sheet of clear glass resting upon two glass bricks, create the illusion of a bountiful harvest of fruits and cheeses without taking an extreme amount of space.*

116

Midsummer's Evening—*Remember the lesson of Walt Disney—just when your company thinks they have had a beautiful, perfect evening, give them more than they were expecting by surprising them with a "little something extra." In New Orleans it's called "Lagniappe." The plus at dinner here was a joking juggler.*

Election Celebration—*Set the stage and the mood with smiles when the host greets his guests dressed in costume to reflect the theme of the party.*

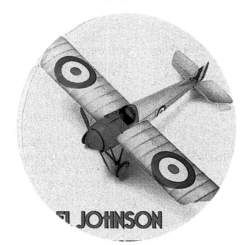

4th of July—*Get everyone involved in expressing themselves with an individual event such as making a button to wear for the party.*

Christmas Eve Dinner & Bar Mitzvah—*Need more space for entertaining—rent a canopy or plan way ahead by building your carport to be a useable outside gazebo to expand for summer entertaining.*

Baby Shower and New Year's Day—*Use a centerpiece other than flowers—arrange accent pieces such as family toys and baby items as was done at the*

Baby Shower or for the Christmas season use glass figures on a mirrored base mixed with lots of candles that make it come alive when lit.

4th of July—*Give a favor that makes the guests remember this fun evening after it's over. Give them an individual wrapped sample of the barbecue sauce you used from the old family recipe. Share a little of your family with them.*

Christmas Coffee—*Make each guest remember this day by giving a Christmas ornament for their tree.*

Superbowl—*Any time you have a football party, or any kind of a party around a T.V. event, have lots of T.V.'s all over the house so the guests can move around during the event. Don't forget the must popular party room, the kitchen.*

Baby Shower—*Make this event a classic with an announcement and prepicture of the baby using ultrasound pictures. This is certainly not your ordinary invitation!*

Dinner Honoring Dr. Shumake—*Use a special event surrounding your group or your charity to reinvolve and reexcite past leaders to keep them active.*

Victorian House Blessing—*Use a non-alcoholic sparkling catawba in fluted champagne glasses so the children attending can be as much a part of the blessing and toasts as the adults.*

Midsummer's Evening—*Make flower arrangements using mostly greenery and flowers from your garden and add a few from the florist.*

Dinner Honoring Dr. Shumake—*Line a large basket with plastic and then fill it with tropical plants and bedding plants that can be planted and reused afterward.*

Election Party—*To be elegant and practical, wrap a linen napkin around a colorful theme paper napkin. The guests can use the paper napkin for lipstick.*

Birthday Party—*Give photo souvenirs. Snap pictures of the guests as they arrive—take them to a nearby one hour photo lab and give them as keepsakes as the guests leave.*

One for the Road—*Give your guests a last surprise—a mug filled with coffee as a favor to take along when they leave.*

Birthday Barbecue—*Wrap the plate, knife and fork, and party favor in a large bandanna to carry out the theme of the party.*

Victorian House Warming—*Do a group of social events back to back to avoid extra preparation and cleaning so you can use the same centerpieces and decorations. The House Blessing was done just after the house was on the Inman Park Tour of Homes.*

Involve the whole family *in party preparation. Under your direction children can cut cookies, roll hors d'oeuvres, chop fresh fruit and vegetables, clean house, and set up decorations so they feel they have contributed to the party.*

Golden Wedding Anniversary—*Use a permanent planted ivy ring on a table and change the flowers in the middle with small pots from the nursery or florist. Also use a display of fresh vegetables as a centerpiece that can be cooked afterward.*

Golden Wedding Anniversary—*Use a simple but elegant symbol repeated throughout the house such as a multitude of gold bows.*

118

LOOKING BACK AT TALLULAH FALLS SCHOOL AND THE CIRCLE

Around the turn of the century, many well-to-do Atlanta families came to the mountains of North Georgia and built summer homes. Their summer colony in the gentle hills was a cool and pleasant retreat from the heat and bustle of city life.

Tallulah Falls Industrial School opened it's doors for teaching on July 12, 1909 with an enrollment of 21 students. Miss Annie Thrasher of Watkinsville was the teacher.

The children from the summer colony near Tallulah Falls played with local children, the descendents of pioneer mountain people. When Mary Ann Lipscomb came to her summer cottage in 1905, she saw that the mountain children who gathered around her cottage were eager to learn to read, and she and other summer visitors began to teach them. She also began to look for a way to establish a permanent school for the area's children.

In the second year the school tripled to three classes.

Mrs. Lipscomb was the president of the Georgia Federation of Women's Clubs, and she appealed to them for help. She told them of families who lived on the steep hillsides, remote from each other and the comforts of civilization. She told them the only schooling that was available for children were classes held occasionally in a room

119

above the jail. She told them of the interest of the area's summer visitors and the efforts of the Moss sisters, who had begun raising money for a fund to build a school. She ended her appeal to the Federation with a resolution that a school be established at Tallulah, and convinced them to take on the project.

The school opened on July 12, 1909 with one class of 21 students, one building, and five acres of land. By the time of its Silver Anniversary in 1934, the school had become known as the "light in the mountains," and an article in the *Atlanta Constitution* said of the success

The School continued to expand and grow when it became a public school for this area reaching a high of over 300 students by its 25th year.

120

of Tallulah Falls School, "It has been done, not by magic, but by faith, courage, and earnest work." And it became a reality because of the dream of a small group of women in a time when they could neither attend their state university nor vote in their state elections.

More than 80 years later, the school had grown to six hundred acres, with 140 boarding students from grades six through twelve.

Mountain children who had no access to public schools were the first students and reason for founding the school.

The school continues to be owned and operated by the Georgia Federation of Women's Clubs, an organization comprised of two hundred clubs with a membership of approximately eight thousand women. Education continues to be a major part of the Federation's activities. In years past, these activities have included working for the enaction of compulsory education laws, establishing model schools in rural districts

In its 80+ years, the School has continued to serve, returning to a private school with 140 boarding students.

that had no schools, establishing kindergartens, and encouraging the formation of school improvement associations. The Federation's other areas of interest are conservation, home life, international affairs, public affairs, and the arts.

The Circle for Tallulah Falls School began when Passie Fenton Ottley was head of the Board of Trustees. In

A Christmas singalong gives a home away from home feeling to the season. Each child receives a wrapped gift from the Circle in addition to the single large gift traditionally given to the school.

1927, she and Mrs. Preston Arkwright formed a group of 75 young women in Atlanta originally called the "Heritage Girls" that later became the Young Matrons' Circle for

Tallulah Falls School. This group, now over 60 years old, has grown to over six hundred members. Through the Circle, many women of prominent Atlanta families and their descendents have contributed time, effort, and personal funds to the

Passie Fenton Ottley was a founder of The Circle, Head of the Board of Trustees, and the wife of John K. Ottley who helped found First Atlanta.

school to buy land, erect buildings, and establish scholarship funds.

In the years since its inception, the Circle has contributed more than $1.6 million to Tallulah Falls School for scholarships and projects as diverse as building a dairy barn, contributing to yearly maintenance costs, building the Passie Fenton Ottley Library, and purchasing a bus. The Circle also has two scholarship funds that provide for students to continue on to college.

122

Tallulah Falls School now has diverse facilities located on 600 acres including it's own operating cattle ranch and dairy barn.

To raise needed capital, the Circle is involved in numerous projects. The biggest of these is the annual Scholarship Ball, held each winter, that now includes a silent auction as well. The Circle has hosted golf tournaments and produced a cookbook. *Culinary Classics,* which sold over sixteen thousand copies. Much of the work and planning for the Circle is done by its board.

Each Christmas, as a way of saying thank you to her board, the president gives a coffee for the 70 members. This year's coffee was given by Liz Sudderth in her home

The Annual Christmas Coffee is a Board favorite. Liz Sudderth, Past Circle President, welcomes members to her home.

One of the things Circle members do well is beautiful entertaining. All the food for this Coffee was prepared by Liz who used to have her own catering business. Her imaginative recipes are included in this book's recipe section.

located in the Atlanta Country Club area of Cobb County. Liz, a former restaurant owner and caterer, sets a beautiful and bountiful table that reflects her professional training. For this occasion, she hired a musician to play piano and sing Christmas Carols so her visitors could (and did!) sing along. Each guest left the party with a lovely Christmas ornament Liz had bought on a trip to Mexico.

As Liz illustrates, one thing Circle members do well is entertain and that became the basis of the newest innovative project, *"Southern Occasions."* This project would

This is a group of Past Circle Presidents at this year's Christmas Coffee.

The Menu

Strawberry Fruit Punch

Coffee

Applesauce Nut Bread

Banana Nut Bread

Baked Ham with Angel Biscuits

Chicken Salad Puffs

Hot Cheese Souffle

Curried Indian Cheese Ball

Artichoke Appetizers

Vegetable Sandwiches &
Cream Cheese Pineapple
Cherry Nut Sandwiches
on Date Nut Bread

Sugared Nuts

Cookies, Fudge, Candy

not have been possible without the help and assistance of the sponsors: First Atlanta, The Westin Peachtree Plaza, and Communication Channels, Inc. which publishes *Business Atlanta*.

GOLD PATRONS

RANDY COTTON / ATLANTA FLORAL ARTS
KERN & COMPANY
LINCOLN NATIONAL DEVELOPMENT CORPORATION

SILVER PATRONS

MARILYN AND NOAH LONG / TRION GROUP
GEWENE WOMACK
MARTHA AND ANTHONY DINOS
EQUIFAX INC.
MAIER & BERKELE
GRUBER & COMPANY, P.C.
CINDY LITES AND RITA ROBB / SOUTHERN DESIGN ASSOCIATES OF
ATLANTA, INC.
PERSIAN GALLERY, INC.
THE RTM FOUNDATION
JAN AND BILL COLLINS/DOGWOOD DESIGNS
LIZANNE AND PETER ABREU
LIZ AND T. SUDDERTH / ACKERMAN REALTY
DOROTHY HAYNES AND J. MITCHELL BOWLING CATERERS
DIANE COOK AND STEPHANIE DIAMOND / ACKERMAN REALTY